May his cry move
us all to do good.

Hamad Bin Khalifa University Press
P O Box 5825
Doha, Qatar

www.hbkupress.com

First published in Arabic by Hamad Bin Khalifa University Press, 2021.
Translation Copyright © Hamad Bin Khalifa University Press.

All rights reserved.

No part of this publication may be reproduced or transmitted in any form or by any means, electronic or mechanical, including photocopying, recording, or any information storage or retrieval system, without prior permission in writing from the publishers.

No responsibility for loss caused to any individual or organization acting on or refraining from action as a result of the material in this publication can be accepted by HBKU Press or the author.

First English edition, 2022

Hamad Bin Khalifa University Press

ISBN: 9789927161001

Printed in Doha-Qatar.

Qatar National Library Cataloging-in-Publication (CIP)

Noun, Mr. author.

[رسالة جرو صغير]. English

Sincerely little fox / by Mr. Noun ; illustrations by Ali Elzeiny ; translated by Ghenwa Yehia. First English edition. – Doha, Qatar : Hamad Bin Khalifa University Press, 2022.

pages ; cm

ISBN 978-992-716-100-1

Translation of: رسالة جرو صغير.

1. Children's stories, Arabic, Translations into English. 2. Picture books. I. Elzeiny, Ali, illustrator. II. Yehia, Ghenwa, translator. III. Title.

PZ10.731. N6813 2022
892.737– dc 23

202228383461

Sincerely, Little Fox

By Mr. Noun

Illustrations by Ali Elzeiny

Translated by Ghenwa Yehia

Little Fox and Baby Fox live in a den, nestled in the heart of the woods. They live there with Mommy Fox.

Mommy Fox is always close by. She has been fiercely protective ever since Daddy Fox disappeared a long time ago.

Sometimes Mommy Fox is lonely, but she hides her tears. Instead, she cuddles close to her cubs during the long winter nights and sings them to sleep.

A small smile plays on her lips. It is shaped like the crescent moon lighting up the sky.

Little Fox looks to Mommy Fox as he dozes off. To him, she is everything.

But one night, darker than any other, a hunter creeps slowly towards the foxes' den.

Shots fired into the darkness. The little fox family wakes up in a panic.

"Run!" cries Mommy Fox to Little Fox.
"Run away – it's a hunter! RUN!"
The last thing Little Fox sees is the fear in their eyes as the hunter drags them away.
Little Fox runs, runs, runs...

He runs through the thick undergrowth of the forest until he reaches the berry trees that mark the edge of the woods. Little Fox has never been so far from home. He can see the tops of the houses where the humans live.

"I am lost," he howls. "Have you seen my mommy and brother? Who can help me? Who?"
But no one answers.

Scared and alone, he ventures down the deserted streets.

In the shop windows, he is confused by what he sees.
A leather wallet that looks like crocodile skin.

A bag and shoes that remind him of his grandmother's silky, soft fur.
A fluffy coat that looks like...!

Could it be?

Heartbroken, Little Fox howls into the night.

"The hunter took my family away to make something to wear.

They put a price on their heads, but do they even care?

My family is priceless, to me but not to you.

Will you ever really truly know the pain you put me through?"

He continues slowly down the street. Peacock feathers woven into a necklace adorn a mannequin's neck. It looks like a brilliantly colored lion's mane.

Another fur stole, red with a streak of white.

"Daddy Fox, is that you?" cries Little Fox.

Little Fox had always hoped that he would meet his lost father and grandparents one day.

But not like this. He did not want to meet them with eyes that do not see and tongues that do not speak.

Silent.

Still.

Dead.

A cold wind sweeps past him and a chill burrows deep in Little Fox's bones.

A roar of thunder rumbles and a streak of lightening pierces the sky. The clouds crack open and sheets of hail rush down.

Little Fox howls at the moon.

The poor cub has been wandering alone for hours now.

When the scent of food reaches his nose, he follows it.

But his hunger only reminds him of Mommy Fox.

"Oh Mommy! What I wouldn't give to be nuzzled against you in our little den in the forest right now!" Little Fox forgets his hunger and settles down in a dark alley, his home for the night.

The little cub sleeps fitfully on the cold concrete bed.

He dreams of his mother.

He longs for her embrace, but he knows it will never be the same.